100

2nd Edition

THINGS TO DO IN THE
TWIN CITIES
BEFORE YOU
DIE

100

THINGS TO DO IN THE
TWIN CITIES
BEFORE YOU
DIE

● ●

TOM WEBER

REEDY PRESS

2nd Edition

Library of Congress Control Number: 2018939880

ISBN: 9781681061573

Design by Jill Halpin

Printed in the United States of America
18 19 20 21 22   5 4 3 2 1

Please note that websites, phone numbers, addresses, and company names are subject to
change or cancellation. We did our best to relay the most accurate information available, but
due to circumstances beyond our control, please do not hold us liable for misinformation.
When exploring new destinations, please do your homework before you go.

CONTENTS

• •

• •

Sports and Recreation

• •

Culture and History

• •

• •

• •

PREFACE

It's awful nice of you to have opened this book; that certainly wasn't necessary, and we kind of expected you'd be too busy to bother. We won't take much of your time. We certainly feel there are so many gosh darn nice things to see around the Twin Cities that someone should have a list of them in book form, but we didn't really want to make you feel pressure to do them.

We Minnesotans are known as a humble, nice, and largely above-average lot who don't care to toot our horn, thank you very much, because the neighbors might be trying to sleep. One of the many jokes about life here in the Land of 10,000 Lakes is that we actually have closer to 15,000 lakes but don't want to brag.

And so it is with that absence of trumpeting I welcome you to my own contribution to Reedy Press's series of 100 Things To Do in various cities before you die. Fear not! I wish you a long life, good health, and many years to complete your bucket list. But there really are some things to you should consider here in the Twin Cities to get the full effect of the Minnesota lifestyle.

This book you're reading is the second edition to a version first published in 2015. Since that time, many things around the Twin Cities have changed—and even a few of the things in the original book have closed! So we thought an update was warranted. But a new book was also necessary after our friends at Reedy saw all the remaining copies of the first book burned in a roaring fire that fortunately only

• •

claimed books and didn't hurt anyone (true story). And so a hearty hat tip also to my friends at Reedy for the gumption they've had these past few months to get this great little publishing house back on its feet. I'm happy to be part of the rebirth in my own little way.

As for life in Minnesota, people in other parts of the country shudder—or maybe shiver—at the thought of our sometimes fierce and long winters and cold. While climate change has actually had a warming effect here, it can still catch you off guard at times. The only way around it is through it; embracing winter will be duly noted in this list. And the rest of the year is so pleasant and near perfect that it's possible our humility and inability to brag is really a well-run conspiracy to keep this place a well-kept secret.

But let's face it—the secret's out. So if you're visiting, recently moved here or are a lifer ready to make sure you're well-stocked in the "to-do" area of life, we're happy to present our 100 things to do in the Twin Cities before you die. And gosh, it's okay if you only get to 20 or 30. We're just pleased you're still reading.

Tom Weber
Updated January 2018

• •

ACKNOWLEDGMENTS

My thanks to Josh Stevens, Barbara Northcott, and Reedy Press for the opportunity to write this book (best of luck to the post-fire Reedy Empire!); to Amanda Doyle, author of *100 Things to Do in St. Louis Before You Die*, who got me started on this path; to all my friends who offered ideas on entries for the top 100; and to Henry and Kate because they're awesome and make it really fun to live here.

FOOD AND DRINK

THE ULTIMATE PATIO RELAXATION
AT WA FROST'S

Minnesotans hate to waste a good summer night, knowing winter is always nigh, and there are few better ways to spend such an evening than dining and drinking outside. Many Twin Cities restaurants offer al fresco seating, but few can match the beauty of WA Frost's in the Cathedral Hill neighborhood of St. Paul. Frost's main restaurant occupies most of the first floor of a historic building (check out the awesome basement lounge). The patio is perfected with a subtle but important decoration: trees. They were never cut down, and the patio appears to have been built around them, leaving an ideal canopy to your night and a great place from which to hang lights. You can't help but relax and have a quiet evening with friends on Frost's patio. Consider reservations on busy nights, but waiting for a table isn't the worst thing either.

WA Frost's, 374 Selby Ave., St. Paul
651-224-5715, www.wafrost.com

HOW ABOUT
A SPOT OF TEA AT MAD HATTER?

In this rough and tumble world that never slows down, there remain a few places where you can get off the merry-go-round for a bit and take a breath.

One such place is the Mad Hatter Restaurant and Tea House in Anoka. Located in the restored 1850s-era Woodbury House along the scenic Rum River, the Mad Hatter is known for great ambiance, a great brunch menu, and of course—the tea! An old-fashioned, high tea service, complete with finger sandwiches and hours of slowing down to visit with friends. No British accent needed!

It has become a popular venue for private events, which is why they recently ended dinner service. But keep an eye out for one-off dinner events, like a Murder Mystery evening or a Valentine's night dinner, which sell out quickly.

Spots available by reservation only! So call ahead and plan your tea getaway in the north metro.

Mad Hatter Restaurant and Tea House
1632 S Ferry St., Anoka
763-422-4160, www.madhatteranoka.com

ENTER THE JUICY
OR THE JUCY LUCY COMPETITION

A truly Minnesotan thing to eat is the Juicy, or Jucy Lucy—a hamburger with cheese melted inside the patty. Many good people have burned their tongues by biting into a Lucy for the first time as the piping hot cheese squirted into their mouths. But once you've mastered how to eat it (less is more with those first bites), you'll never think of regular hamburgers the same.

Two Minneapolis eateries claim to have invented the marvel: Matt's Bar and the 5-8 Club.

Your task: try both. We'll reserve judgment here. Just note this: at Matt's, they spell it "JUCY LUCY" (without the *i*); 5-8 spells it "JUICY LUCY," so your very spelling might show favoritism.

President Obama ate at Matt's in 2014, but he never made it to 5-8. Was that a presidential endorsement in this battle, or do we consider his opinion not fully informed?

Matt's Bar & Grill, 3500 Cedar Ave., Minneapolis
612-722-7072, www.mattsbar.com

The 5-8 Club, 5800 Cedar Ave. S., Minneapolis
612-823-5858, www.5-8club.com

TIP

Seriously, be careful the first time you bite into this burger.

EAT WITH BEARDS
(BEARDS NOT REQUIRED)

The Twin Cities has a wickedly awesome food scene. An impressive cornucopia of most kinds of ethnic foods is available; the locavore movement is robust, and there's even a healthy food truck scene.

But it's not just the quantity of food. Several Twin Cities restaurants have won the prestigious Beard Award in recent years, and several more were among the nominees. The Beards are considered the Academy Awards for restaurants . . . or maybe the Oscars should be considered the Beards for movies.

This to-do item is simple: find a way to eat at most of these award winners and nominees soon. Your palate will thank you.

They include the famed Kramarczuk's, Al's Breakfast (item #8), 112 Eatery, Alma, Manny's Steakhouse, the Bachelor Farmer, Tilia, Butcher & The Boar, Salty Tart, Barbette, Marvel Bar, Rustica, Sea Change, D'Amico, Travail, Young Joni, Spoon and Stable, and Heyday.

Look them up here
www.jamesbeard.org/awards

CHOOSE YOUR OWN
BEER ADVENTURE

Recent years have seen an explosion of local craft breweries and brewpubs, thanks to a 2011 law that allows brewers to sell their beer on-site.

So many good beers are now being made across the Twin Cities that you would never be able to sample them all in one effort. So be creative: plan a beer trip to visit several breweries, either by geographical area (walkable sections of town with several breweries) or mode of transport (by bike or light rail).

This entry won't do justice to the growth of the beer scene in the Twin Cities. And it just keeps growing! One way to keep up with so much to explore is the Minnesota Craft Brewers Guild, an organization with an extensive list of who's out there and worth your visit. They also host several events, including the wildly popular "Land of 10,000 Beers" event in the Agriculture/Horticulture building during the Minnesota State Fair. Drink responsibly!

Minnesota Craft Brewers Guild
www.mncraftbrew.org

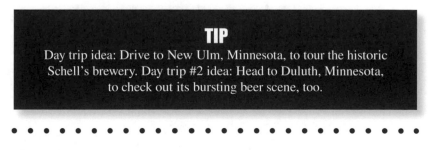

TIP
Day trip idea: Drive to New Ulm, Minnesota, to tour the historic Schell's brewery. Day trip #2 idea: Head to Duluth, Minnesota, to check out its bursting beer scene, too.

A STEAK AND AN OLD-FASHIONED

AT THE OLD-FASHIONED MANCINI'S

If you like steak, there's no point in reading any further. Put down this book and head to Mancini's Char House & Lounge, a St. Paul institution. You can't get more meat and potatoes than this place. And you can't get more retro either.

This place drips with character just the way the garlic bread drips with butter. Not much of the decor has been updated since Mancini's debuted in 1948, and we like it that way. When you're done with dinner, head into the large lounge for an old-fashioned and enjoy some karaoke or the musical devotions of the golden band, the Midas Touch, a Mancini's regular for decades.

Come for the steak, stay for the ambiance, and raise your glass to a truly bygone era.

Mancini's, 531 W. 7th St., St. Paul
651-224-7345, www.mancinis.com

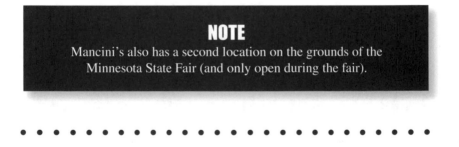

NOTE
Mancini's also has a second location on the grounds of the Minnesota State Fair (and only open during the fair).

HISTORICAL NOTE

Mancini's had, for several decades, a contemporary in the iconic Nye's Polonaise in northeast Minneapolis, another uber-retro restaurant with its own house band called the World's Most Dangerous Polka Band. Nye's closed its doors in 2016; however, a smaller "tribute" Nye's opened in early 2018 and aims to capture some of the magic of the original with a few original features and a mural including founding owner Al Nye.

SAMPLE FOOD ON A STICK
AT THE STATE FAIR—DAILY

This list would not be complete without the iconic state fair, also known as the Great Minnesota Get-Together. This item blends two challenges people have: to attend the fair all twelve days of its annual run and to eat a lot of food on a stick. It's the iconic food: something portable and thus on a stick.

Maybe it's bacon on a stick one day, cheesecake the next, a pancake breakfast the third, or tater tot hotdish the fourth. You make your own list of what to eat, and there are new offerings every year. Plenty of sticked samples are available to allow for a daily dose if you're game for twelve trips to the fair. Are you? No one will ever doubt your true Minnesotan cred.

Minnesota State Fair Food
www.mnstatefair.org/find/food

TAKE PART
IN A BREAKFAST DINER RITUAL
AT AL'S BREAKFAST

There's a counter at Al's Breakfast with fourteen stools. And that's about it (the place is only about ten feet wide). This Dinkytown mainstay near the University of Minnesota campus is your chance to take part in a morning ritual that dates back almost sixty-five years. The diner appears to have been built in what used to be the alley between two buildings.

Assuming that all the stools are in use when you get there, just stand along the back wall and wait (eavesdropping is allowed). Once seated, try the pancakes or waffles and be ready to move. The good folks at Al's want to make sure parties of two or three can sit together, so you might need to scooch. It's cool. We're all in this together.

Al's Breakfast, 413 14th Ave. SE, Minneapolis
612-331-9991, www.alsbreakfastmpls.com

MUSIC AND ENTERTAINMENT

SPEND HALLOWEEN
IN THE HALLOWEEN CAPITAL OF THE WORLD

The good people of Anoka, Minnesota, take their Halloween seriously. So much so that the north metro suburb has been designated as the Halloween Capital of the World. The World, people!

City fathers first scared up nearly a month of activities back in 1920 as a way to deter kids from pranks! Idle hands, you know. Now, Anoka fills October with events, including dances; bingo; a high school football game called the Pumpkin Bowl; and one of the largest parades in the state, a staple in the community for decades.

Consider running the Gray Ghost 5K Run before the parade, but wear a costume—you'll run faster.

Recognizing the degree to which Anoka takes seriously its Halloween, the U.S. Postal Service in 2016 announced it would issue Halloween-themed stamps for the first time in its history, and it would mark that occasion in Anoka.

Anoka Halloween
www.anokahalloween.com

PENUMBRA THEATRE

For the scores of theater options that exist in the Twin Cities, make sure one of them is the Penumbra Theatre in St. Paul. Penumbra is one of a handful of professional African American theaters in the nation that offer full seasons of shows.

While the theatre itself is unassuming—it shares space with a community center next to a park in the Cathedral Hill neighborhood of St. Paul and seats fewer than three hundred people—the cozy settings and stage add a certain intimacy to the important topics the shows are sure to explore. Penumbra wades into any and all issues surrounding race and the African American experience in the United States and lays it bare on the stage.

Whether it's a series of adaptations of plays by the famed August Wilson, an important look at the life of Nat King Cole, or a captivating look at daily life in black America with a show literally called "Two Old Black Guys Just Sitting Around Talking," no topics are off limits for Penumbra, and you'll appreciate that when you go.

Penumbra Theatre, 270 N. Kent St., St. Paul
651-224-3180, www.penumbratheatre.org

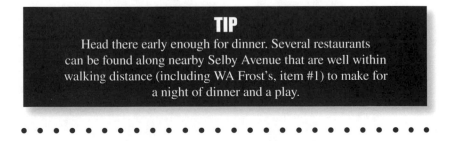

TIP
Head there early enough for dinner. Several restaurants can be found along nearby Selby Avenue that are well within walking distance (including WA Frost's, item #1) to make for a night of dinner and a play.

PLAY SOME OLD-FASHIONED HOCKEY
AT THE U.S. POND HOCKEY
CHAMPIONSHIPS

For Minnesotan hockey lovers, the idyllic vision of learning to play as a kid on any random patch of ice comes to life every winter with the U.S. Pond Hockey Championships on Lake Nokomis in Minneapolis. With an aim to play hockey the way it's meant to be played, as organizers proclaim, grown men and women spend a full weekend outside in January playing hockey.

The game is near-Norman Rockwellian. Players must shovel the ice themselves before each game (no Zambonis). Teams of four try to score on goals made of plywood and boards (think of kids using an old crate). There are refs but no checking, slap shots, or even goaltending. If you can flick the puck into that small opening in the box-goal, you deserve the point.

Players of all skill levels enter, so consider dusting off your old skates and scraping together a team. Or, just attend.

US Pond Hockey Championships, Lake Nokomis, Minneapolis
www.uspondhockey.com

GET YOUR MOVIE FIX
AT AN ACTUAL MOVIE THEATER

If cable and Internet service ever go out in the Twin Cities, you'll be fine. The Twin Cities host several film festivals each year that you should attend. The biggest and best known is the Minneapolis-St. Paul International Film Festival, which lasts most of April and features more than 150 films from dozens of countries. The event simultaneously prides itself on its international flair and also a homegrown smattering of movies with Minnesota connections. Most movies are screened at the St. Anthony Main Theatre in northeast Minneapolis.

But film fests don't end there. Also check out the Twin Cities Film Fest (different than the Minneapolis-St. Paul International Film Fest), the Twin Cities Black Film Festival, Twin Cities Arab Film Fest, Twin Cities Jewish Film Festival, the only known Hmong film festival in the world, and the Minneapolis Underground Film Fest, to name just a few.

**Minneapolis-St. Paul
International Film Festival**
612-331-7563
www.mspfilm.org

Twin Cities Film Fest
www.twincitiesfilmfest.org

Twin Cities Black Film Festival
www.facebook.com/tcbff.org

Twin Cities Arab Film Fest
www.mizna.org/arabfilmfest

Twin Cities Jewish Film Fest
www.tcjfilmfest.org

Minneapolis Underground Film Festival
www.mplsundergroundfilmfest.com

Qhia Dab Neeg Film Festival
https://filmfreeway.com/festival/QhiaDabNeeg-
FilmFestival

GO WILD
AT THE MINNESOTA AND COMO ZOOS

Two zoos are located in the Twin Cities, each with its own distinct feel and each worth a visit. The Minnesota Zoo is an expansive, state-run menagerie in suburban Apple Valley. St. Paul Como Zoo sits in the heart of Como Park; it's smaller and older and free! Both have added upgrades in recent years, including Russia's Grizzly Coast at Minnesota Zoo and the new Gorilla House at Como.

And don't forget the animals! Lions, tigers, and bears, indeed. And bugs, birds, sea otters, tortoises, flamingoes, and giraffes. The World of Birds show at the Minnesota Zoo is not to be missed, and neither is the storied Sparky the Sea Lion show at Como. The Como Zoo is also adjacent to a beautiful conservatory to appease your need for tropical flowers (especially in the winter). In non-winter months, the Japanese garden is not to be missed.

Minnesota Zoo (admission charged), 13000 Zoo Blvd., Apple Valley
952-431-9200, www.mnzoo.org

Como Zoo (free admission), 1225 Estabrook Dr., St. Paul
651-487-8201, www.comozooconservatory.org

PRO TIP

Go to the Minnesota Zoo in the
spring when its Zoo Babies program features
the most adorable critters; the zoo's summer
concert series is also worth it. And make sure
to utilize Como Zoo's April Fool's Hotline next
April 1 to trick your friends into calling
Mr. Lion or Ms. Ella Fint.

RIDE THE RAILS
FOR A TWIN (AND SAINT) BILL

The Twin Cities has the potential for baseball fans to see two games in two cities on the same day. The Green Line (light rail) starts at Target Field in Minneapolis—home of the Minnesota Twins—and ends at Union Depot in St. Paul's Lowertown neighborhood. From the depot, it's a long walk from the bullpen to the St. Paul Saints' minor league ballpark.

Your task: check the Twins' and Saints' schedules to find a date when both teams are home and have staggered enough start times (day/night?) to allow you to watch one game, board the train, and then travel to the other park to see the second. This kind of whirlwind Baseball Day already is possible in such cities as Chicago and New York—and now the Twin Cities.

The fun part is that there might be years with no workable dates, making the double bill all the rarer to accomplish and all the more satisfying to achieve. And keep an eye out for comedian Bill Murray at the new Saints' ballpark; he's part owner of the team.

Minnesota Twins, Target Field, 353 N. 5th St., Minneapolis
612-659-3400, www.minnesotatwins.com

St. Paul Saints, CHS Field
651-644-6659, www.saintsbaseball.com

Green Line (light rail transit)
612-373-3333, www.metrotransit.org

FLOCK TO FIRST AVENUE

The history of the robust Twin Cities' music scene will always prominently include the venue First Avenue. Built in a former Greyhound bus station in downtown Minneapolis, First Ave (you'll stick out if you pronounce the entire word "avenue") rose to national prominence with the 1984 release of the cult classic film *Purple Rain*. The movie stars the late, great Prince, one of Minnesota's favorite sons, and was released about a month after his wildly successful album of the same name.

Many scenes in the movie take place inside First Ave, and nostalgic fans have flocked to the venue ever since. But they've also flocked for the music. First Ave's still very much a working concert venue. So find a show on the schedule and spend an evening in close quarters with your fellow music lovers. Snap a selfie outside along the wall of stars, featuring the names of performers who have graced the First Ave stage.

Upon Prince's untimely death in 2016, fans flocked to a huge street concert in front of First Ave to pay respects, along with his home and recording studio in Chanhassen, Paisley Park, which now operates as a museum (www.officialpaisleypark.com).

First Avenue, 701 N. 1st Ave., Minneapolis
612-332-1775, www.first-avenue.com

SEE HOW MANY FRINGE SHOWS
YOU CAN PACK IN
AT THE MINNESOTA FRINGE FESTIVAL

Ever wonder if your coworker Gary from HR is also an amazing performer? He might be performing in the Minnesota Fringe Festival, the largest non-juried fringe festival in the nation. An explosion of performing arts, this event showcases over eight hundred performances of more than one hundred fifty hour-long shows, happening over eleven days at various venues across Minneapolis.

It's structurally impossible to see every show, so choose wisely. The fest is slotted by lottery, meaning there's a wide range of talent on deck. Okay, let's stop sugarcoating: some shows are real duds. But many are brilliant! The fun of the Fringe Fest rests largely in picking shows and figuring out how to race from venue to venue to catch the next one. Spend a full Saturday or Sunday immersed in Fringe. And when you find a dud, embrace it. Organizers say the lemons are the shows people most remember.

Minnesota Fringe Festival
612-872-1212, www.fringefestival.org

HAVE A GRAND OLD DAY

Celebrate the start of summer with a quarter million of your best friends. That attendance mark has the organizers of Grand Old Day in St. Paul claiming to be the largest one-day festival in the Midwest.

St. Paul's Grand Avenue is already known as a can't-miss boulevard of restaurants and shops, but for more than forty years, the first Sunday of every June has seen twenty blocks opened to more than food and merchandise vendors along with several stages with live music.

The event includes a parade down Grand on Sunday morning. Show up for the floats; stay for the food and festivities.

Grand Old Day
www.grandave.com/grand-old-days

HMONG FREEDOM
CELEBRATION

In the Twin Cities, the Fourth of July weekend doesn't just include fireworks and parades. The Hmong Freedom Celebration and Sports Festival has graced St. Paul summers for more than thirty years.

Known also as "J4," this family-friendly, two-day event in Como Park draws upwards of sixty thousand people from across the world.

Minnesota is home to the nation's second-largest population of Hmong Americans. Hmong music, food, sport, dress, and pageantry are all on display. And the games! Don't miss the huge soccer tournament, and watch a few games of kato, a popular sport in Southeast Asia that's also known as sepak takraw. The game resembles volleyball except you can't use your hands. Players often kick the ball over the net with impressive moves.

Hmong Freedom Celebration and Sports Festival
651-221-0069

ENJOY DINNER
AND A SHOW—WITHOUT MOVING!
AT CHANHASSEN DINNER THEATRES

An evening at the Chanhassen Dinner Theatres will leave you wondering why the trend of dinner theaters went out of style. Your admission buys you an entree from the menu (served before the show) and then the evening's entertainment. Show up early for a drink in the Hogarth Lounge while you wait to be seated for dinner. There are three theatres, in all, each offering a different performance.

Two of them—the Main and Playhouse theatres—serve dinner in the same room as the performance. Patrons of the Fireside theatre will eat their meal in a separate room, then retire to the theatre for the show.

There's also a summer musical theatre camp for students.

Chanhassen Dinner Theatres
501 W 78th St., Chanhassen
952-934-1525
www.chanhassendt.com

BE AWED BY
THE COWLES CENTER

The Cowles Center in downtown Minneapolis is a one-stop venue for all things dance in the Twin Cities. Ballet, modern dance, interpretive—it's all there on the especially-with-dance-in-mind stage. Attending a show will make you sorry you ever gave up tap when you were a kid, but that's a normal feeling.

While pondering your own dance what-ifs, take a moment to consider the architecture: the building incorporates the Shubert Theater, which was famously (and slowly) moved in its entirety over twelve days down Hennepin Avenue in 1999. Modern meets must-keep in architecture terms.

Cowles Center for Dance and the Performing Arts
528 Hennepin Ave., Minneapolis
612-206-3600, www.thecowlescenter.org

SET NEW STANDARDS
AT THE DAKOTA

It's a cold Minnesota winter night. You dodge snowbanks on Nicollet Mall and duck into the Dakota Jazz Club, where a full menu promises to meet your every nosh-worthy craving. And just as you finish your meal, feeling contented and a little drowsy, out come the performers to give you a smooth set that we swear really does help with digestion.

The Dakota couldn't be a more intimate setting. Check out their website for their extensive list of guests and reserve your seat now.

If you're a fan of jazz, it won't be long before your time in the Twin Cities includes a trip to the Dakota. The same can be said if you're a fan of good food.

Dakota Jazz Club, 1010 Nicollet Mall, Minneapolis
612-331-1010, www.dakotacooks.com

SPEND HALLOWEEN
IN THE WOODS

Consider spending your next Halloween walking through dark woods to an outdoor puppet show that probably includes a few fires. What could possibly go wrong?

For more than twenty years, the group BareBones Productions has performed an outdoor Halloween pageant on the grounds of some Twin Cities park—usually Hidden Falls in St. Paul. The show has grown in popularity, though organizers still consider it a cult favorite.

The point is to use puppetry, drama, fire, and music to take note of the important connection that Halloween (and autumn) have to the end of life (and the seasons). There's even a chance for audience members to call out and remember those who've died. And at the end, enjoy a free feast of food and drink.

Despite the prominent use of fire, regulars will tell you to bring a blanket and a thermos of something warm (exact item is up to you).

It's truly a unique spectacle not to be missed; it usually runs for a few nights leading up to Halloween.

The Annual Halloween Outdoor Puppet Extravaganza
by BareBones Productions
www.barebonespuppets.org/halloween-show

FRANCONIA
SCULPTURE PARK

You could lose hours wandering the twenty-plus acres of art at the Franconia Sculpture Park, not far from Taylors Falls in the St. Croix River Valley.

It's hard to describe the towering, larger-than-life sculptures you'll see here, in part because there's always something new. The art is quirky and innovative. Some defy explanation; others make you want to write poetry.

Most of the sculptures are hands-on and sometimes climb-on. Get a snack from the concession stand built into a giant lizard, and then walk through the park possibly hearing the sounds nearby of welders and carpenters creating the next installation. If you go to the Franconia Sculpture Park tomorrow, head back in six months to see what's new.

The park is free and open from sunup to sundown every day of the year.

Franconia Sculpture Park, 29836 Saint Croix Trail, Shafer
651-257-6668, www.franconia.org

SEE BOTH ORCHESTRAS,
INSIDE AND OUT

The Twin Cities is the rare metropolitan area that hosts not one but two major and renowned orchestras. Both the Minnesota Orchestra and St. Paul Chamber Orchestras are Grammy winners, and both have performance spaces that have recently undergone major renovation work.

Orchestra Hall sits along Nicollet Mall in downtown Minneapolis. The Ordway Center for the Performing Arts in downtown St. Paul is a dynamic presence overlooking Rice Park. Check out both new digs, but also look for outdoor events. These have included Minnesota Orchestra shows at the Lake Harriet Bandshell and SPCO shows at Mears Park. A perfect, family-friendly reason to bring a picnic and hear actual world-class music.

Minnesota Orchestra
www.minnesotaorchestra.org

St. Paul Chamber Orchestra
www.thespco.org

A NIGHT OF MUSIC
AT THE TURF CLUB

One of the most unique music venues in the Twin Cities is the Turf Club in St. Paul. Billed as the "best remnant of the '40s," the dive bar/hole-in-the-wall/trendy spot has, in recent decades, become a must-go for live music lovers. With a capacity of around three hundred, it makes for an intimate night of music.

Turf now draws an impressive roster of names from the indie rock scene, especially since it was bought (and renovated) in 2013 by First Ave (see item #15). While doing that renovation work, crews discovered a horse-racing-themed mural that's now on display. Other than that, no frills. And while you're there, head downstairs to the jazz spot known as the Clown Lounge, named for its clown-themed light fixtures and artwork that adorns the walls. If you're genuinely scared of clowns, maybe skip this room.

Turf Club, 1601 University Ave. W., St. Paul
651-647-0486, www.turfclub.net

GO MEDIEVAL
AT THE RENAISSANCE FESTIVAL

Minnesotans have been traveling back to the 1500s for more than forty years now in what has become the largest Renaissance Festival in the country—three hundred thousand people can't be wrong! Based in suburban Shakopee, the fest runs weekends from late August into October. Bring your dog!

It's enough just to see the fashion and jousting, but there's so much more: sixteen stages with live entertainment fit for a king, including the storied Puke & Snot show. Keep an eye out for some of the street acts, like Beefcake & Olive (you might hear them before you see them) and the Royal Court. Hundreds of booths have real craftsmanship on display (and for sale). Plenty of food is available, and consider a sample of the adult beverage mead—wine made with honey instead of grapes—which is made on-site.

This is an all-day, family-friendly event that happens rain or shine.

Minnesota Renaissance Festival, 12364 Chestnut Blvd., Shakopee
952-445-7361, www.renaissancefest.com

TRIVIA

The famed comedy magic duo Penn & Teller
performed as a pair for the first time in 1975
at the Minnesota Renaissance Festival.

MAY DAY PARADE

The May Day Parade is unlike any other parade of the summer. The puppets are a big reason for that, but so is the festive atmosphere you never quite experience anywhere else.

The event started in the mid-1970s as a thank-you gift, of sorts, from In the Heart of the Beast Puppet and Mask Theatre to the south Minneapolis community for its support. It's now a year-round event where artists and volunteers make puppets large and small to tell a loose-knit story around the year's themes. If you don't help out and march in the parade yourself (no motorized vehicles allowed), then at least be in the audience.

Thousands line Bloomington Avenue to see the creative puppets that range from the handheld to the gigantic and from the adorable to sometimes scary.

If puppets aren't your thing, stick around for (or march in) the "Free Speech Section" of the parade—just bring a cause you support and a banner!

The parade ends with a ceremony and festival in Powderhorn Park. Puppets and humanoids unite!

May Day Parade, In the Heart of the Beast Puppet and Mask Theatre
www.hobt.org/mayday

APPLAUD MINNESOTA'S BEST AMATEUR TALENT
AT THE MINNESOTA STATE FAIR
AMATEUR TALENT CONTEST

Performing in a talent show might conjure memories of some fourth grade pageant where it all went wrong, but now you can exorcise those demons with a trip to the amateur talent contest at the Minnesota State Fair, a fixture for more than forty years. These people deserve to be onstage!

Minnesotans from across the state who have won previous shows either at the state fair or at a county fair are there to sing, dance, play instruments, juggle, or do something called pizza acrobatics (an actual thing). It's a wide range on the entertainment spectrum with three categories—PreTeen, Teen, and Open. The best part is knowing the performers are regular joes and janes who might live next door.

Thousands attend each year at the State Fair Grandstand. Cheer on your neighbors, or sign up yourself! We'll cheer you on!

Minnesota State Fair Amateur Talent Contest
www.mnstatefair.org/entertainment/talent_contests.html

THE SLEDS JUST ALL FALL APART
AT ART SLED RALLY

Another way to beat winter is to throw yourself down a hill atop flimsy cardboard or so the organizers of the Art Sled Rally in Powderhorn Park believe.

Held on the third Saturday in January, come snow or snow, all are invited to make a sled (and that's a liberal use of the word "sled") with cardboard or any other materials from your home, and run it down on a cordoned-off hill in Powderhorn Park in south Minneapolis. Spoiler alert: very few sleds make it intact. If laughing were a fuel, though, they'd go for days. You don't get any points for actually getting anywhere.

Coordinated by a group of residents in the Powderhorn Park area and artists who go by the name South Sixteenth High Jinks, the real majesty is the art and effort in creating elaborate sleds. Past creations included an aquarium filled with sledders dressed as various sea life; a replica of London's Tower Bridge; and various game recreations, such as Pac Man and Hungry Hippo. You really have to see it in person. It's a spectacle, and for a few hours we all forget it's winter.

Art Sled Rally
Powderhorn Park Neighborhood Association, 821 E. 35th St., Minneapolis
612-722-8640, www.artsledrally.com

FEEL
THE NORTHERN SPARK
AT NORTHERN SPARK

It starts at 9 p.m. and goes until sunrise. Northern Spark is an all-night art festival one night a year—outdoors—in mid-June. You can't help but feel giddy and ready for summer with a trip there.

Organizers pick main spots in the Twin Cities to unleash the art gods. Basically, you can't walk five steps that night without running into the next temporary exhibit, whether that's performance, light shows, art on display, or the time that guy built a cardboard house and then set it on fire in the wee hours (true story).

In some ways, Northern Spark is for the lazy art consumer. You will take in so much art in one night that you could argue you're set for the rest of the year. It's an electric and eclectic event not to be missed.

Northern Spark
http://northern.lights.mn/platform_group/northern-spark/

GET INTO
THE CHRISTMAS SPIRIT
AT ST. OLAF

If you need music to get into the Christmas spirit, don't look for those stations playing "Jingle Bells" all day. Instead, head an hour south of the Twin Cities to Northfield for the St. Olaf Christmas Festival at St. Olaf College. They've only been doing it for, you know, more than a century (since 1912).

More than five hundred student musicians who are in one of five choirs and the St. Olaf orchestra take part. They perform individually and as an impressive mass ensemble. The event gets national acclaim and broadcast, but being there in person is the real treat, especially for the finale, "Beautiful Savior."

There are only a few performances, in early December, so be ready to snag your seat when tickets go on sale in October.

St. Olaf Christmas Festival, St. Olaf College
1520 St. Olaf Ave., Northfield, www.christmas.stolaf.edu

PRO TIP
Get there early enough to take a leisurely walk through the campus before heading to the Skoglund Center Auditorium for the performance.

THE BUFFALO DO ROAM
AT BELWIN CONSERVANCY

Hey, remember before European settlers arrived and there were probably more bison around than you could count? And then remember when those settlers killed all the bison?

Funny story: It turns out those bison are actually really important contributors to the health of the prairies and native grasses that existed millennia before Minnesota did.

And so we suggest a trip to see a few efforts to bring back the bison. A non-profit called the Belwin Conservancy—which works to conserve and restore land in the east metro and St. Croix Valley—places bison in their prairies to let them be bison and help restore the land (something about rolling around in the dirt is very helpful).

Head out to the observation platform Belwin set up for Joe Q. Public near Afton. The bison are only there during the warm months of the year, but give them a gander. And remember: Sometimes bison just lie around. Don't expect a show. They're just being bison.

Bison Observation Platform, Belwin Conservancy
Intersection of Stagecoach Trail S & Division Street, Afton, MN
651-436-5189, www.belwin.org/bison/

NOTE
If you're up for a road trip, two other places in Minnesota with bison are Minneopa State Park near Mankato and Blue Mounds State Park near Luverne.

CELEBRATE CINCO DE MAYO
IN THE WEST SIDE

Head to the west side of St. Paul for the annual Cinco de Mayo Celebration, a one-day, family-friendly event. In addition to a parade along Cesar Chavez Street and live music, you should consider entering jalapeno-eating contests (go for it). Then check out the impressive cars in the low-rider car show, a one-of-a-kind show that includes low-rider bikes! It's a rain or shine event, and it's free.

Cinco de Mayo West Side Celebration
www.cincodemayosaintpaul.com

SPORTS AND RECREATION

THESE AREN'T YOUR
PARENTS' CAMPER CABINS

The Twin Cities has an enviable mix of regional, city, and state parks, allowing for moments of zen without a long drive. But not everyone has embraced his or her inner outdoorsiness and might pause at the thought of even one night in the woods without creature comforts.

Not to worry! The park systems are on it. Take Dakota County Parks, for example. They've installed three modern, sleek cabins in the woods of Whitetail Woods Regional Park in Farmington. These cabins are as close to glamping (glamour camping) as you'll find. Each cabin has lights, heat, even wifi and a ceiling fan! And of course a fire pit for the rustic in all of us. They're beautifully built to merge well with the surrounding woods—even won a big architecture award a few years back! Each cabin holds up to six people, but at less than $100 a night you could spring for a solo or couples trip.

After that, feel free to move a little more rugged with the yurt, available at Afton State Park in the east metro. No electricity but great wood-burning stoves to keep you warm (as long as you keep feeding the fire). Yurts are insulated canvas tents with wood floors—no need to sleep on the ground!

In both cases, cabins and yurts must be reserved and are very popular, so check the websites for availability.

**Whitetail Woods Regional Park—
camper cabins!**
17100 Station Trail, Farmington
952-891-7000
www.co.dakota.mn.us/parks

Afton State Park—yurts!
6959 Peller Ave S, Hastings
651-436-5391
www.dnr.state.mn.us/state_parks

NATURE, CENTERED

The Twin Cities region has an impressive collection of nature centers. Like our equally impressive collection of parks, nature centers offer trails for hiking and picnic opportunities. But they're also especially catered to families and school groups, with plenty of day camps and other activities for humans of all ages. We'll highlight a few nature centers here—but this isn't a complete list! Keep an eye out for nature centers in your part of the region.

Tamarack Nature Center in White Bear Township features a cool nature play area called "Discovery Hollow" that is essentially a playground without slides or swings. Wear a swim suit and play in the stream (learn to make a dam!) or build a tree fort or climb the cliffs or just play in the mud at the mud table!

Westwood Nature Center in St. Louis Park has 160 acres of marshland, prairie and woods just 10 minutes from downtown Minneapolis. Check out the puppet shows for preschoolers and have a kids birthday party there and hold an exhibit animal. Wildlife!

Dodge Nature Center in West St. Paul—one of the first nature centers in Minnesota—offers summer camps, displays of farm animals and raptors, and even includes plots you can rent to grow your own garden or even rent a space to keep bees!

Tamarack Nature Center
5287 Otter Lake Rd., White Bear Township
651-407-5350
www.ramseycounty.us/residents/parks
-recreation/tamarack-nature-center/play
-outdoors/discovery-hollow-play-area

Westwood Nature Center
8300 W. Franklin Ave., St. Louis Park
952-924-2544
www.stlouispark.org/government/
departments-divisions/parks-rec/
westwood-hills-nature-center

Dodge Nature Center
365 Marie Ave, West St. Paul
651-455-4531
www.dodgenaturecenter.org

NEED A SAUNA?
THEY'RE PORTABLE NOW

Minnesotans have enough Scandinavian immigration in their histories that we embrace a hearty number of elements of Nordic life in the North (see Lutefisk, item #72). One such experience is the sauna. Aside from the usual roster of gyms and clubs with saunas, people with means often install saunas at their homes or cabins to enjoy during the winter months.

But what about the rest of us schlubs who can't afford that? Behold! Now you can visit a sauna—a portable one.

A group called the 612 Sauna Society has constructed a sauna on a trailer—think of a big U-Haul trailer but equipped with sauna-ness. The Society parks the sauna at a fixed spot for a few weeks— they call it a residency—and you can sign up online to reserve a two-hour spot. They've so far had residencies at the American Swedish Institute and at Surly Brewing Company.

The Society is also a co-op, so you can be an owner-member of this little Nordic experiment (but you don't have to be a member to sign up for a sauna appointment). The head honchos proclaim that this the first co-op sauna in the nation. Yes, please! And no nudity! Bring your bathing suit and some water to stay hydrated and let go of your day.

612 Sauna Society—check website for locations/reservations
www.612saunasociety.com

DITCH THE CAR
FOR NICE RIDE MN

Minneapolis and St. Paul often top (or nearly top) rankings for bike-friendliest cities in the country. Just about any activity in this book can be reached by bike. In addition to miles of urban routes, most lakes and rivers (including the mighty Mississippi) are lined with paths, and getting anywhere is quite possible on a bike—even in the winter when the most hardy souls use fat tires.

If you don't have a bike, rent one. The Twin Cities is among the ever-growing number of metros with a bike rental program (ours is called Nice Ride MN). With just a little practice, you'll find it possible to fill an entire weekend with outings you can get to on two wheels. Don't forget your helmet!

Nice Ride MN
www.niceridemn.org

LUMINATE YOUR WINTER
AT LUMINARY LOPPET

Minnesota winters can be famously harsh, which is what makes the Luminary Loppet one of those breathtaking experiences that make you *feel* Minnesotan. It's a short ski jaunt—at night—across one of the Twin Cities' most scenic lakes—Lake of the Isles. The groomed ski path is lined with thousands of luminaries—candles inside little vases made of ice—and a host of "rest stops" for snacks and entertainment (including fire dancers). There are no electric lights on the lake—just the glow of thousands of candles to guide you as you blend your true Minnesotan desire to walk or ski on frozen lakes (perfectly normal in these parts) with that most primal need to interact with neighbors when many retreat to the solitary comfort of heated homes.

You can't help but feel calm, at peace, and happy at this very family-friendly event. No skis? No problem. You're simply asked to walk (or snowshoe) alongside the groomed ski paths.

If you want a quintessential Minnesota experience, sign up early for next winter's Luminary Loppet.

Luminary Loppet, Lake of the Isles, Minneapolis
612-604-5330, www.loppet.org/luminary-loppet

NOTE

The Luminary Loppet is one of several events held during a weekend of ski racing activities that range from supercompetitive to not-at-all-competitive (like the luminary), so make sure you're signing up for the right event online.

APPRECIATE THE RIVER
AT THE MISSISSIPPI NATIONAL RIVER AND RECREATION AREA

The histories of Minneapolis and St. Paul are nothing without rivers. The Mississippi begins as a trickle in Lake Itasca State Park in northern Minnesota (worth the trip) and flows through its first major metropolitan area at Minneapolis-St. Paul.

But for all the 2,320 miles of river from Minnesota to the Gulf of Mexico, the Twin Cities is the only section of river that's also a national park, the seventy-two-mile Mississippi National River and Recreation Area.

Head to the park's headquarters in St. Paul (in the Science Museum, item #76) to learn about all the activities to be had on this specially designated stretch.

Look for hidden hikes along the river too. We suggest Hidden Falls Regional Park, with breathtaking views of the river, bird-watching, and some serious thinkin' time.

Mississippi National River and Recreation Area
Visitors Center: 120 W. Kellogg Blvd., St. Paul
651-290-4160, www.nps.gov/miss/index.htm

TOUR BOTH CITIES
BY BIKE ON CONSECUTIVE WEEKENDS

For a comprehensive view of both Minneapolis and St. Paul by bike, sign up for the Minneapolis Bike Tour and the St. Paul Classic Bike Tour. They each offer loop courses between fifteen and forty-five miles, and they're usually planned on consecutive weekends. So why not try *both* next year? The events include live bands, rest stops, and support and gear vans if you get a flat.

Several segments of each event are also along closed or partially closed roads, giving you unique views of the cities often only seen by car. Thousands of your neighbors take part in this family-friendly event; join them!

Minneapolis Bike Tour
www.minneapolisbiketour.com

St. Paul Classic Bike Tour
www.bikeclassic.org

GUSH OVER
MINNEHAHA FALLS

There's something magical about a waterfall in the center of a major metropolitan area. Minnehaha Falls drops water fifty-three feet at a point inside one of Minneapolis's oldest city parks. Hundreds of thousands of annual visitors (and at least two sitting presidents) have taken in the awesome sight and then maybe grabbed a bite at the nearby restaurant Sea Salt.

The falls rarely disappoint. They slow to a trickle during droughts (a placard near the falls reveals that when President Lyndon Johnson visited in 1964, fire hydrants were opened to "create" a falls). But there's usually a nice, steady flow to whisk you into a moment of urban meditation.

And you needn't wait for summer: the sight of the frozen falls in winter, if not chilly, is an impressive sight for which smartphone cameras were invented.

4801 S. Minnehaha Park Dr., Minneapolis
612-230-6400
www.minneapolisparks.org/parks__destinations/parks__lakes/
minnehaha_regional_park/

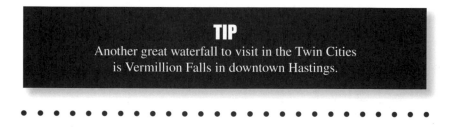

TIP
Another great waterfall to visit in the Twin Cities
is Vermillion Falls in downtown Hastings.

PRO TIP

Walk along Minnehaha Creek after the falls for that last mile before it empties into the Mississippi River. The creek there is shallow and popular for fish-seeking birds, such as the great blue heron. The hiking paths can flood and be slippery when the water levels rise, so take note. But if the paths are dry, walk all the way to the Mississippi and add another mark to your Minnesota Experiences punch card.

KAYAK THE ST. CROIX

Three major rivers traverse the Twin Cities—the Mississippi, the Minnesota, and the St. Croix. The Mississippi gets most of the glory, but the St. Croix deserves some love. It's a stunning tributary that starts in Wisconsin and spends much of its life as the Minnesota-Wisconsin border. As a National Scenic Riverway, the St. Croix enjoys protections that limit motor boats and jet skis in many places. That leaves a river with stunning natural views and the serenity with which to enjoy them. You'll forget how close you are to a major metropolitan area when you rent a kayak or canoe and amble down the river without a care in the world.

Two popular spots to rent canoes are at Interstate State Park at Taylors Falls, Minnesota, and Wild River State Park near Hinckley, Minnesota. Bring some food for a picnic; several places are available along the way to stop and watch the river. A swim can be refreshing, but be careful of the current, especially if it's been a rainy season and water levels are higher.

Interstate State Park (MN)
Milltown Road, Taylors Falls, MN
www.dnr.state.mn.us/state_parks/interstate/index.html

Taylors Falls Rentals, via Wild Mountain
651-465-6315
www.wildmountain.com/taylors-falls-canoe-kayak-rental

Wild River State Park
39797 Park Trail, Center City, MN
www.dnr.state.mn.us/state_parks/wild_river/index.html

Wild River Rentals, via Eric's Canoe Rental
651-270-1561
www.ericscanoerental.com/index.html

PRACTICE YOUR TRIPLE AEXEL
AT WINTERSKATE AND THE OVAL

Explore your inner figure skater with wintertime rinks open to ice dancers of all ages and skill levels. In St. Paul, head to WinterSkate, an ice rink erected each winter next to the Landmark Center. In Roseville, head to the Oval, an outdoor rink open in winter next to the year-round indoor Roseville Ice Arena.

Both places have skate rentals—WinterSkate happens amidst a wonderful view of downtown St. Paul. Plenty of people head there for a quick skate on their lunch hours.

Lace up and invigorate your winter with a few laps on the ice.

WinterSkate, 75 5th St., St. Paul
612-749-0435
www.wellsfargowinterskate.com

The Oval, 2661 Civic Center Dr., Roseville
651-792-7007
www.skatetheoval.com

SCREAM YOUR HEAD OFF
AT VALLEYFAIR

This would be a fantastic time for you to get over your fear of roller coasters. Some of the rides at Valleyfair in suburban Shakopee have perfected that feeling of your gut falling away from your shoulders. The Corkscrew and Wild Thing are popular rides, and the Power Tower offers a lovely view from two hundred seventy-five feet above the Twin Cities' suburbs—for about two seconds—before plunging you back to earth.

But for many, it's the High Roller—Valleyfair's classic wooden roller coaster, which debuted in 1976 along with the rest of the amusement park. The oldies really are the goodies.

Also head over to the Soak City waterpark and cool off on a hot summer day.

Valleyfair, 1 Valleyfair Dr., Shakopee
(952) 445-7600, www.valleyfair.com

GO BECAUSE YOU CAN
TO CAN CAN WONDERLAND

If you're in need of a sensation overload—and maybe a rum-filled malt with Cap'n Crunch cereal sprinkled atop—head to the wacky mini-golf/vintage arcade/live event space that is Can Can Wonderland.

Built in an old, repurposed factory in an otherwise nondescript industrial part of St. Paul, Can Can has harnessed the power of the Twin Cities art scene to make an incredible playground for kids and adults alike.

One main attraction to Can Can is its peculiar mini golf course—each hole designed by a local artist. One hole requires a putt into a State Fair Ferris Wheel; another has you maneuver a retro living room; and then there's the baseball hole, where you actually hit your golf ball with a kids bat. Aim for the fences!

Then there's the Boardwalk Arcade, featuring a roster of vintage arcade games. And the event space for live music and other entertainment. And if this overstimulation gets to be too much for parents trying to keep track of their kids, never fear! Parents! Order that bizarre-sounding malt that's spiked with some liquid courage.

Can Can is open Thursdays through Sundays to all ages until 9 pm, when it becomes an age 21+ playground.

Can Can Wonderland, 755 Prior Ave. N, Suite #004, St. Paul
651-925-2261, www.cancanwonderland.com

CHEER ON THE RUNNERS
AT THE TWIN CITIES MARATHON

If you want to run a marathon, you absolutely should. It's a great accomplishment. But if you're not all that keen to learn where your body most easily chafes, consider at least watching the Twin Cities Marathon.

Held on the first Sunday in October, spectators and runners will know they've treated the weather gods well if they awake to a brisk morning that becomes a beautiful fall day. The course of the marathon showcases the Twin Cities—starting in downtown Minneapolis, weaving along lakes, creeks, and rivers and over to St. Paul up its iconic Summit Avenue with a triumphant finish line at the State Capitol (item #69).

As a spectator, any spot along this course is a great place to set down a lawn chair and marvel at the work it takes to train for a marathon. Runners genuinely appreciate the cheering masses that motivate them to the end. You won't get a medal for cheering, but you'll have done your part.

Twin Cities Marathon
651-289-7700, www.tcmevents.org

WALK ON THE WATER
OF A FROZEN LAKE

The idea of walking on a frozen lake might sound haunting and scary . . . at first. But then that hardy, Minnesotan, let's-beat-winter drive takes over. Make sure your time in the Twin Cities includes a walk across a frozen lake.

Yes, it's freezing and usually very windy, but if you're bundled up, there's also something very peaceful about standing in the middle of a lake (especially at night) and feeling a little removed from the rat race. The tongue-in-cheek rule about lake walking is "Never Be the First Person to Walk on a Lake."

Take special care when lakes are first freezing in the winter and thawing in the spring. At the height of winter, though, and at the height of below-freezing temperatures, an ice jaunt will be uneventful.

Consider also the scattering of events during the winter that take place on frozen lakes, such as the Kite Festival on Lake Harriet in Minneapolis (which also has ice fishing demonstrations).

LAWN BOWLING
AT BRIT'S

Everything about Brit's Pub in downtown Minneapolis is British, from the ales on tap to the fish 'n chips on the menu, but head upstairs to the rooftop level and take in, or play, a game of lawn bowling. It's an easy enough game for anyone to learn. It resembles Bocce; players roll their bowls, as they're called, closest to the jack.

There are open hours every weekend for any Johnny-come-latelies. Another option is to join a lawn bowling league, but Brit's website proclaims to have a ten-year wait list! Sure, playing a no-stress game with your friends while sipping a pint is enticing, but now add in the backdrop of the downtown Minneapolis skyline on a warm summer evening, and you'll understand why this rooftop attraction is a can't-miss.

Brit's Pub Lawn Bowling, 1110 Nicollet Mall, Minneapolis
612-332-3908, www.britspub.com/lawn_bowling/

WALK YOURSELF
AROUND THE U

The University of Minnesota, established in 1851, is older than the state of Minnesota and has many fine, old buildings to prove it. Don't let another summer go by without a self-guided walking tour of the campus. The Minneapolis campus sits on both sides of the Mississippi River, and you could easily spend an entire day exploring.

One place to start is Pillsbury Drive, a row of the U's oldest buildings. A stroll starts at the Armory and heads along the impressive Pillsbury Hall, with its stones and arches. Other landmarks along Pillsbury include Nicholson Hall, Eddy Hall, and Burton Hall, along with the underground Williamson Hall, a newer structure built underground. Just off Pillsbury Drive is the glorious Northrop Hall, visible on your walk.

University of Minnesota
www.umn.edu

WANDER SWEDE
HOLLOW

Swede Hollow is not St. Paul's largest park, but its unique layout in a deep ravine begs for a visit. It also has a colorful, if not checkered history.

Home for decades to St. Paul's poorest immigrants, the final residents were evicted and the buildings were burned in the 1950s.

Swede Hollow then became a woodland with a few visible signs of its history in a few corners. Walking and biking paths guide your visit, and you're not too far from the Bruce Vento Nature Sanctuary (item #53), so head there after you've taken in Swede Hollow.

If you're wondering what the huge abandoned-looking, fenced-off factory is at the northern end of the park, that's the former Hamm's Brewery. Flat Earth, a new brewery, is one of the new occupants.

Swede Hollow Park
www.stpaul.gov/facilities.aspx?page=detail&rid=97

HELP COUNT THE BIRDS
AT THE CHRISTMAS BIRD COUNT

We're a bird-loving bunch, we Minnesotans. So much so that the local Audubon Society has, since 1905, hosted an annual Christmas Bird Count. Volunteers sit outside for a few hours every December and literally count (and identify) the birds that go by.

This falls under one of those "greater good" categories. Yes, it's largely a volunteer effort, but because it's happened for more than a century, the data have become essential for researchers.

Even though it happens at the height of winter and you don't get paid for your time, the spots usually fill up. Bring your binoculars!

Christmas Bird Count, Minnesota Ornithologists' Union
www.moumn.org

BIKE TO STILLWATER
FOR LUNCH

A trip to Stillwater is a must. Nestled along the idyllic St. Croix River, downtown Stillwater is a perfect place to spend the day antiquing, shopping, and eating. But now consider really earning it: grab your bike and ride the twenty-ish mile trip there!

Take the Gateway State Trail, which starts about a mile or so from the State Capitol in St. Paul. A picture-perfect, tree-canopied trail, you'll rue the day you ever thought to drive to Stillwater! Near Highway 96, pick up the Brown's Creek State Trail for the final six miles into Stillwater.

If a forty-mile round-trip on a bike sounds daunting, make this your summer challenge. Start training in the spring, and plan for your trip in early fall!

PRO TIP
Put a spin on this idea and build in a night
at a Stillwater B&B to the trip.

BRUCE VENTO
NATURE SANCTUARY

One of the best features of the Twin Cities is a healthy supply of spots that seem far removed but are actually just a few steps from a major city center. One of those is the Bruce Vento Nature Sanctuary, a twenty-seven-acre patch of land just outside the edge of downtown St. Paul that is a true escape.

It's an escape even though you can clearly see the downtown St. Paul skyline, and you can hear trains from the rail yard next door. But the sanctuary is also perfectly situated at the base of a bluff that makes you feel cozily nested. Ducks usually hold court in the ponds on the eastern end of the sanctuary, and several good sittin' rocks are around for one to ponder life.

Bruce Vento Nature Sanctuary, 4th St. E., St. Paul
651-266-6400, www.stpaul.gov/facilities/bruce-vento-nature-sanctuar

IF YOU CAN'T ARBORETUM
JOIN 'EM

The trees are your friends, as you'll learn with a trip to suburban Chaska to visit the University of Minnesota Landscape Arboretum. More than eleven hundred acres of lush trees and plants await you year-round. Check out the twenty-eight gardens, including the rose, Japanese, and waterfall gardens, and take the bog boardwalk through a wetland. The Arboretum is an easy place to get lost in with the wandering trails (wheelchair access is limited in some areas); you'll come home with plenty of garden tips. You can also venture by car, though the main road closes to cars in winter.

The cafeteria is good for lunch; lots of windows look out on the landscape.

Minnesota Landscape Arboretum, 3675 Arboretum Dr., Chaska
952-443-1400, www.arboretum.umn.edu

PRO TIP
Come back in the winter to use sixteen miles
of cross-country ski trails.

PADDLE A CHAIN
OF LAKES

Along the northeast shoreline of Lake Calhoun in Minneapolis, you should rent a kayak or canoe or paddleboard or boat and course your way through three of the five lakes that comprise the famed Chain of Lakes. Head immediately to the canal under Lake Street that connects Calhoun to Lake of the Isles (home of the Luminary Loppet, item #38). Take in the views of the beautiful houses as you keep along the west edge of the lake. Then take the canal under Lake of the Isles Parkway that connects to Cedar Lake. That canal will be an idyllic paddle along backyards. On Cedar Lake, turn right and head over to Hidden Beach for a swim.

Lake Calhoun Rental, via Wheel Fun Rentals
3000 Calhoun Parkway East, Minneapolis
612-823-5765, www.wheelfunrentals.com

A ROLLERING GOOD TIME
AT THE ROLLER DERBY

One of the most family-friendly evenings in the Twin Cities (and plenty of other cities across the country) is Roller Derby. Yes, roller derby. The sport has seen a resurgence in the past decade, with leagues popping up across the globe.

Newcomers will be confused by teams of women roller skating in a loop, crashing into each other and falling down a lot. But stay with it; ask someone nearby for a lesson about jammers and how to score points; and you'll quickly learn it's a sport of finesse and great athleticism.

Just about everyone you see—from the athletes to announcers to referees—is volunteering. Athletes (who make up their own stage names) spend down time skating through the venue to visit with fans and even help at the face-painting booth. It's really about the roller derby, man!

In the Twin Cities, there are two leagues that each feature several teams: The Minnesota RollerGirls in St. Paul and North Star Roller Derby in Minneapolis. The RollerGirls teams compete at the historic Roy Wilkins Auditorium in downtown St. Paul; North Star teams are at the Warner Coliseum on the Minnesota State Fairgrounds.

Check them out and be prepared for a dance party at halftime.

Minnesota RollerGirls
Roy Wilkins Auditorium (called The Roy)
175 W Kellogg Boulevard, Suite 501, Saint Paul
www.mnrollergirls.com

North Star Roller Derby
Warner Coliseum, Judson Ave. & Clough St.
Falcon Heights
www.northstarrollerderby.com

LEARN TO CURL
AT THE ST. PAUL CURLING CLUB

The winter sport of curling seems to captivate the nation every four years at the Olympics (in 2018 nearly every member of Team USA's men's and women's teams were from Minnesota). But don't just wonder what those brooms are for—learn to sweep on the ice yourself at the St. Paul Curling Club, the oldest curling club in Minnesota.

Players throw stones or rocks down sheets of ice, trying to get closest to the house—a circular target on the ice. The game is all finesse, and the brooms play a big role in how the rocks turn or slow down or don't slow down. Take in a few games at the club, and then inquire about joining a league and try your hand. And don't be surprised to see some Olympians playing on the sheet next to you. Good curling!

St. Paul Curling Club, 470 Selby Ave., St. Paul
651-224-7408, www.stpaulcurlingclub.org

CRASHED ICE

Nothing like a truly extreme sport to heat up winter, and we can confirm the Red Bull Crashed Ice event in St. Paul has both crashing and ice.

It's become a popular draw. Several thousand people come out on cold nights in January to watch competitors skate down a twisting course of ice. The track is temporary, built in the shadow of the iconic Cathedral of St. Paul. The sport, officially called ice cross downhill racing, combines hockey, downhill skiing, and the luge.

You can try out (and sign a lot of waiver forms) if you want, or you can all but eliminate your risk of a broken leg by just watching in person. Dress warmly and marvel at the extremes sports have attained.

Red Bull Crashed Ice, Selby & John Ireland Blvd., St. Paul
www.redbullcrashedice.com

HEAD TO THE
(CHLORINATED) SWIMMIN' HOLE

For a state with more than 10,000 lakes, it might seem preposterous to propose a day at a manmade lake filled with chlorinated water. But the swim pond has become a popular concept for families with small kids as a bridge between pools and lakes.

The Three Rivers Park District has swim ponds at two parks: Lake Minnetonka Regional Park in Minnetrista and Elm Creek Park Reserve in Maple Grove.

These ponds, open from Memorial Day to Labor Day, have all the trappings of a beach — a sandy lake bottom, big beach umbrellas, lifeguards, concessions, and nearby playgrounds. But the water in the ponds is filtered and chlorinated; depths are cordoned off so you have an idea of how far to let kids go; and there's no seaweed or icky things to step on. This lets families with little ones dip their toes into lake life a little earlier.

The hearty Minnesotan might harrumph and yell to just jump in the darn lake. But some of the stress of carting a young family around open water is quelled with these "starter lakes." And fear not, hearty Minnesotan. With the Lake Minnetonka swim pond, the actual Lake Minnetonka is just a few steps away when you're ready to make the jump.

Lake Minnetonka Swim Pond
4601 County Road 44, Minnetrista
763-694-7754
www.threeriversparks.org/location/lake-
minnetonka-swim-pond

Elm Creek Swim Pond
12420 James Deane Pkwy., Maple Grove
763-694-7894
www.threeriversparks.org/location/elm-
creek-swimming-pond

FLOAT ALONG
MINNEHAHA CREEK

Another watercraft must is tubing Minnehaha Creek. There are no rental places along the creek, though, so you'll have to use your imagination to procure an inner tube or rent a kayak or canoe from a local outfitter. Minnehaha Creek runs twenty-two miles from Lake Minnetonka (item #59) to the Minnehaha Falls (item #41). Pick a segment along that stretch to lazily let the currents take you downstream. The creek runs through backyards in Edina but mostly parkland in Minneapolis—a little bit for everyone! Bring a picnic and find a spot to have lunch along the way.

Minnehaha Creek Watershed District
www.minnehahacreek.org

PRO TIP

This can be a tricky outing to plan if the creek levels are too high or too low. Keep an eye on notices from the Minnehaha Creek Watershed District.

CULTURE AND HISTORY

DO FARM CHORES
AT THE KELLEY FARM

Sure, your own laundry sits undone, but that shouldn't stop you from heading to the Oliver H. Kelley Farm to help them with their chores!

This is one of those places that sneak in good old-fashioned learning by covering it with fun. Located in suburban Elk River on land once owned by Oliver H. Kelley, visitors can see firsthand a hint of what it was like to live on a farm in the 1850s, when this part of Minnesota was still very much frontier land.

Kelley is best known as founder of the national farming organization known as the Grange. It's a working farm; staff wear period clothing and invite visitors to help with gardening, field chores, cooking, and other tasks. You can go from plowing a field to making molasses to learning the history of agriculture in a few hours. Parents: the farm is a popular school field trip, so you might end up being taught by your own children when you go.

And don't forget the farm animals! The oxen seem to be the big draw for kids. As one former employee noted, it's "crazy how throwing in an ox makes kids beg to do chores." We do not recommend getting an ox as a motivator for your own home chores. The farm is open from Memorial Day to Labor Day.

Oliver H. Kelley Farm, 15788 Kelley Farm Rd., Elk River
763-441-6896, www.mnhs.org/kelleyfarm

SEE A GAGGLE OF FIRE TRUCKS
AT THE FIREFIGHTERS HALL & MUSUEM

Is that the proper term for a group of fire trucks? A flock? A pack? A parliament? Whatever the word, there's a nondescript building in northeast Minneapolis that houses at least ten fire trucks from throughout the history of firefighting in Minnesota. It's all part of the Firefighters Hall & Museum, a labor of love for a dedicated group of volunteers (many are retired firefighters) who run the place.

Visitors of all ages are welcome to climb on some trucks and take part in interactive firefighting exhibits. During summer months, the museum offers rides on some of the vintage trucks! It's also a popular space to rent for kids parties (if you're looking for ideas).

Because it's volunteer-run, the museum is only open on Saturdays. But it's well worth the trip, especially if someone in your family is mesmerized by the sight and sound of fire trucks.

The building also houses historical items if you're looking to research the history of the Minneapolis and St. Paul fire departments. And there's a sobering exhibit called "81 Minutes" that details how first responders answered the call to one of the most significant moments in recent Twin Cities history: The 2007 collapse of the I-35W bridge.

Firefighters Hall & Museum, 664 22nd Ave. NE, Minneapolis
612-623-3817, www.firehallmuseum.org

• •

GO ON A TREASURE HUNT IN ST. PAUL
... REALLY

Another way to beat winter is to crawl through it . . . while looking for the St. Paul Pioneer Press Medallion. The treasure hunt dates back to the 1950s and coincides with the St. Paul Winter Carnival. St. Paul's daily newspaper, the *Pioneer Press*, posts clues once a day for up to twelve days for where to find the medallion.

It's buried somewhere, usually a park, in Ramsey County. But it's more complicated than that. The medallion is often buried very well, including being encased in ice, resting inside the pocket of a pair of jeans, or taped to a food canister and buried in snow. It's not uncommon to hear about people taking off work to search, but they have a great motivation: the reward for finding the medallion is as much as $10,000. Vacation day, anyone?

St. Paul Pioneer Press Treasure Hunt
www.twincities.com/treasurehunt

List of previous medallion locations:
www.twincities.com/treasurehunt/ci_22395861/
pioneer-press-treasure-hunt-medallion-locations

SPAN
THE STONE ARCH BRIDGE

One of the most iconic images of the Twin Cities is the downtown Minneapolis skyline, which features one of the Mississippi River's most unique bridges—the Stone Arch Bridge. Featuring twenty-three arches of stone and built for trains by railroad baron James J. Hill (see item #91) in the 1880s, it opened for pedestrians and bikes only in 1994, offering the best view yet of St. Anthony Falls and the skyline.

It's easy to spend an evening on and around the bridge or an entire weekend! Father's Day weekend is now set aside for the Stone Arch Bridge Festival, which features art and music on the St. Anthony side of the river, with a perfect view of the bridge.

Stone Arch Bridge, 1 Portland Ave., downtown Minneapolis
www.minneapolisparks.org
www.nps.gov/miss/planyourvisit/stonarch.htm

RUIN A DAY
AT MILL CITY MUSEUM

We know we're asking a lot here, but trust us when we say one of your best family outings will be a museum dedicated to flour that includes an elevator as a main highlight. Stay with us: modern Minneapolis history is forever tied to the Mississippi River, whose sheer force at St. Anthony Falls was harnessed to provide water for a burgeoning flour industry that would shape the nascent city's future.

The Washburn-Crosby Company (later known as a little company called General Mills) built its first mills along the river in the 1880s. After a fatal explosion that leveled several mills in 1878, a new Washburn A Mill was opened in 1880 and produced the famed Gold Medal Flour until 1965. That building, left vacant for decades, was gutted by a massive fire in 1991.

But making lemonade out of lemons, the Mill City Museum was built inside the burned ruins. Marvel at the architecture, but don't miss the Flour Tower, a tricked-up elevator ride that offers a vertical view (with recreated machinery) of how the mill's floors once looked. And don't miss the observation deck atop the building, with stunning views of the falls. On your way out, grab free samples of whatever's being made in the Baking Lab. Exhibits also show the history of iconic brands like Pillsbury (and its famed doughboy mascot, Poppin' Fresh), Wheaties, and Bisquick.

Mill City Museum, 704 S. 2nd St., Minneapolis
612-341-7555, www.millcitymusuem.org

● ●

PRO TIP

Head there during the summer on a day when the museum is hosting a concert in its courtyard—the best place to see the mill's ruins—and enjoy a soundtrack to your visit.

RIDE HISTORIC STREETCARS
AT THE MINNESOTA STREETCAR MUSUEM

Like many cities, the Twin Cities had an extensive streetcar network in the early twentieth century that fizzled as cars became ever more en vogue. Fortunately, a stretch of track remains between Lakes Harriet and Calhoun in Minneapolis, where you can enjoy the clang clang of the trolleys through a scenic wooded area.

Some trolleys date back more than one hundred years, and the Minnesota Streetcar Museum operates them during warm weather months. All streetcar operators are serious train buffs who volunteer their time (and have proper training as streetcar drivers). The ride is just a few minutes, but if you're lucky, the memories last forever.

Hours are seasonal and trips canceled when it rains to protect the restored streetcars. This is super family-friendly attraction, but the old streetcars have limited capacity for people with disabilities, so contact them ahead of time with questions.

Como-Harriet Streetcar
www.trolleyride.org

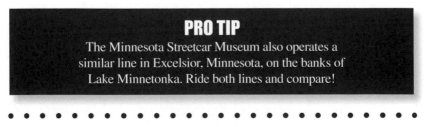

PRO TIP
The Minnesota Streetcar Museum also operates a similar line in Excelsior, Minnesota, on the banks of Lake Minnetonka. Ride both lines and compare!

RIDE HISTORIC STREETCARS
... ON THE WATER

Once you tackle item #66, do the same thing on the waters of one of Minnesota's best-known lakes! Take a cruise (weekends and holidays during warm weather months) of Lake Minnetonka on a "streetcar boat" fashioned to look like old streetcars and originally used to transport residents across the lake. After that era, the boats were scuttled.

But one of them, now called Steamboat Minnehaha, was dredged from the bottom of the lake and restored in the 1980s.

In its heyday, Lake Minnetonka (and its amusement park that no longer exists) was the terminus of an oft-traveled streetcar line. The streetcars remain, with one on land in Excelsior and one on water. Climb aboard!

Steamboat Minnehaha
www.steamboatminnehaha.org

FIND THE END
OF THE ENDLESS BRIDGE
AT GUTHRIE THEATRE

As noted in item #64, the downtown Minneapolis skyline is a must. But where's the best vantage point? We suggest the Guthrie Theater's Endless Bridge. A cantilevered lobby that extends one hundred seventy-eight feet from the building face, the endless bridge is a dramatic and exquisite spot.

Most of the bridge is indoors, with windows the designer framed to force your view on certain landmarks, according to Guthrie's website. The final part of the bridge is outdoors, giving you that panoramic river view.

The Guthrie theater building, perched along the riverfront, actually houses three theaters that are open year-round to performances, but you don't need a show ticket to still walk inside and take the escalator to the endless bridge. The attraction acts almost as a fourth theater, with the Minneapolis riverfront as the stage. Plan to spend considerable time thinking and taking pictures here.

Endless Bridge, Guthrie Theater, 818 S. 2nd St., Minneapolis
612-377-2224, www.guthrietheater.org

TOUR
THE STATE CAPITOL

One of Minnesota's architectural marvels is its State Capitol. Famed architect Cass Gilbert designed some of the nation's first skyscrapers and the U.S. Supreme Court building in Washington, D.C., but his work on the Minnesota Capitol arguably put him on the map nationally.

It opened in 1905 as the state's third capitol building. The best view is from the rotunda looking up into the massive and breathtaking dome (one of the largest self-supporting marble domes in the world). You should also stand on the front steps and look out on the extensive capitol grounds, along with perfect views of downtown St. Paul and the impressive Cathedral of St. Paul. If you come during the legislative session, you're sure to see a rally trying to raise attention for a cause. Join a cause!

Minnesota State Capitol, 75 Rev. Dr. Martin Luther King Jr. Blvd., St. Paul
651-296-2881, www.mnhs.org/capitol

PRO TIP
Head to the Capitol on Minnesota Statehood Day—May 11—to see the huge chandelier at the top of the rotunda lit. It's only lit on statehood day and rare, special occasions!

HAVE A JOLLY GOOD TIME
AT THE BRITISH ARROWS

We Minnesotans sure do enjoy the adverts those Brits put on the telly. Our friends across the pond have for nearly forty years bestowed awards called the British Arrows on the best ads in their land, and for nearly thirty years, the Walker Art Center in Minneapolis has hosted screenings of the award winners.

The ads range from the dramatic to the inventive to the tear-jerking and heartwarming to the laugh-out-loud, make-you-cry-with-laughter ingenious.

The British are coming . . . with their ads . . . and you should be happy about it.

British Arrow Awards at the Walker Art Center
1750 Hennepin Ave., Minneapolis
612-375-7600, www.walkcrart.org

SEE LIFE-SIZED PRINCESSES CARVED IN BUTTER
AT THE MINNESOTA STATE FAIR

Head to the Dairy Building at the Minnesota State Fair and behold the wonders of the butter princesses. Each year the Midwest Dairy Association holds the pageant known as "Princess Kay of the Milky Way." Princess Kay and her court, who all hail from dairy families, each get their likeness carved into ninety pounds of butter.

They and the butter sculptor sit in a small rotating refrigerated booth for nearly six hours in the Dairy Building while we gawk at the wonder of butter art.

Butter Princesses!
Dairy Building, Minnesota State Fair
Corner of Judson & Underwood
www.midwestdairy.com/schools-and-communities/dairy-princess/
princess-kay-of-the-milky-way/

TRY
THE LUTEFISK

Every hardy Minnesotan really should try lutefisk at least once. Stemming from the state's deep Scandinavian heritage, lutefisk is a fish entree (often cod) prepared by being soaked in lye and steamed. It's a highly mocked dish because, well, so many people find it disgusting. The general rule is that lutefisk (pronounced LOO-teh-fisk) is only swallowable (never mind tasty) if drenched in butter.

Lutefisk has its defenders, though, and the world's largest lutefisk processor is in Minneapolis! There's something to be said for a staple that remains a staple even when it's unloved. Lutefisk is like Scandinavia's fruit cake, and if Minnesotans don't embrace it, who will?

Several churches, VFWs, and community centers serve lutefisk during fall and holiday season events, so a quick Internet search should yield a nearby event. The Annual Lutefisk Dinner at Mount Olivet Lutheran Church in Minneapolis, for example, is usually held the first Friday in December and dates back to 1929. More than twelve hundred pounds of the fish are served; it's not clear how much butter is consumed.

THE ST. PAUL
MUSEUM TOUR

Downtown St. Paul includes three impressive and family-friendly museums. The Minnesota History Center, Minnesota Children's Museum, and the Science Museum of Minnesota are a few blocks' walk from each other. We've grouped them in this book for those ambitious souls who might want to try all three in a day, but it's fine if you want to slow things down a bit and give them all their due.

Minnesota History Center, 345 Kellogg Blvd. W., St. Paul
651-201-6000, www.minnesotahistorycenter.org

Minnesota Children's Museum, 10 W. Seventh St., St. Paul
651-225-6000, www.mcm.org

Science Museum of Minnesota, 120 W. Kellogg Blvd., St. Paul
651-221-9444, www.smm.org

MINNESOTA
HISTORY CENTER

From a history of toys (!), to a look at 1960s Minnesota, to a forty-year retrospective of our vibrant Hmong community, the Minnesota History Center is your go-to place to learn all things Minnesota. Very family friendly with two great stores offering Minnesota wares, the museum has temporary exhibits and permanent displays, such as an interactive look at a Minnesotan's favorite topic: weather. Also check out the moving re-creation of a World War II combat flight inside a military plane in the Minnesota's Greatest Generation area.

And if you go on a Tuesday afternoon in July or August, bring a picnic and stay for an outdoor evening concert.

Minnesota History Center, 345 Kellogg Blvd. W., St. Paul
651-201-6000, www.minnesotahistorycenter.org

MINNESOTA
CHILDREN'S MUSEUM

Your only mission at the Minnesota Children's Museum is to play yourself into an impressive nap time. The multifloor spread in downtown St. Paul wants you (and your children, we suppose) to learn by way of playing. The youngest toddlers can crawl around the Sprouts while older kids can act out the things adults do, like shop for groceries, stock a hardware store, or be a postman in the Our World room.

Head to Imaginopolis, where you can build forts, arches, and your imagination skills.

And don't miss the Scramble! A four-story climbing extravaganza that opened when the museum expanded a few year ago. There's a spiral slide and a very high catwalk to maneuver (no shoes, please!).

Parents are almost universally thankful for this indoor playground during winter months.

Minnesota Children's Museum, 10 W. Seventh St., St. Paul
651-225-6000, www.mcm.org

SCIENCE MUSEUM
OF MINNESOTA

A hands-on, family-friendly explosion of science, you'll go from dinosaur bones and an Egyptian Mummy to learning about the human body by looking at your own cells under a microscope, topped by learning something big in an omnitheater screening. You can also learn about the Mississippi River either from a museum's exhibit, by stopping by the National Park Service's river visitor center, or by looking out the back window, where the river flows by. Make up a song on the musical stairs and, in the summer, learn about rivers and erosion as you play a round of mini golf in the Big Yard.

Science Museum of Minnesota, 120 W. Kellogg Blvd., St. Paul
651-221-9444, www.smm.org

NOTE
The museum became a sensation in late 2017 when the show *Stranger Things* included episodes where a character wore a retro hoodie sweatshirt that the museum sold as a T-shirt in the 80s... a purple shirt with a brontosaurus on it. The museum couldn't keep them in stock around the holiday shopping season!

CHERRY SELFIES
AT THE SCULPTURE GARDEN

One of the Twin Cities' iconic images is a huge sculpture of a spoon holding a cherry, with the downtown Minneapolis skyline in the background. That installation, called *Spoonbridge and Cherry*, is the best-known spot inside the Minneapolis Sculpture Garden.

More than forty pieces of public art fill this peaceful eleven-acre garden, which is perfect for strolling and sitting. Once you find the spoon and cherry (which is also a fountain), try trick photography. Stand far enough away to frame a photograph with you in the foreground that gives the appearance of you holding the spoon and eating the cherry. Test your photo skills!

But wait! The spoon and cherry have competition, it appears. With the Garden's reopening in 2017 after a massive restoration, visitors appear pretty drawn to the giant blue rooster called *Hahn/Cock*. So don't be chicken! Look for the rooster and all the other new pieces that debuted with the garden's reopening.

Minneapolis Sculpture Garden, 725 Vineland Pl., Minneapolis
www.walkerart.org/visit/garden

THE NEWBORN ANIMALS ARE ADORABLE
AT THE MIRACLE OF BIRTH CENTER

A key reason the Minnesota State Fair is truly the state's get-together is the livestock shows that bring high schoolers (and their families) from across the state to showcase their prized cows, sheep, goats, poultry, and even llamas. But for those animals in no condition to walk around, head over to the Miracle of Birth center to see farm life's debut.

With veterinarians on hand if needed, visitors can't help but view either a live or taped birth being shown on one of the many monitors throughout the building. Yes, birthing is messy and a healthy cacophony of "ewwws" season the soundtrack of the moment, but your heart will melt with the opportunity to see (and pet) the cleaned-up critters—including baby chicks and sheep!—as they ponder their existence during farmland's version of the debutante ball.

Miracle of Birth Center (During MN State Fair)
www.mnstatefair.org/entertainment/ag_exhibits/chs_mob.html

HAVE DRINKS
ATOP THE FOSHAY

The Foshay tower is easy to spot; it's the one with the big word "FOSHAY" across the top. It's staggering to imagine that, for a time, Foshay was the tallest building west of the Mississippi River.

It was completed in 1929, just a few months before its namesake, Wilbur Foshay, lost everything in the stock market crash.

The architectural marvel reopened as a hotel in 2008. Head to the Prohibition Bar on the twenty-seventh floor for a cocktail and take in the panoramic views amidst impressive woodwork. A museum and observation deck are on the thirtieth floor. That deck is not wheelchair accessible and not always open during winter, so call ahead.

Foshay Museum & Observation Deck, 821 Marquette Ave., Minneapolis
612-215-3783, www.wminneapolishotel.com/foshaymuseum

Prohibition Bar
612-215-3700, www.wminneapolishotel.com/prohibition-bar-minneapolis

SEE JESSE JAMES IN NORTHFIELD
DURING THE DEFEAT OF JESSE JAMES DAYS

Drive about an hour south of the Twin Cities to the charming town of Northfield. Part of the charm is its quaint downtown of shops and restaurants and being home to not one but two small liberal arts colleges, St. Olaf and Carleton. The town's motto is "Cows, Colleges & Contentment."

Consider also a summer trip to relive the history of Jesse James. The James/Younger gang's ill-fated robbery of Northfield's First National Bank in 1876 is reenacted every summer at the Defeat of Jesse James Days, complete with raid, shootout, and getaway.

Defeat of Jesse James Days, Downtown Northfield
www.djjd.org

TOUR
THE GOVERNOR'S MANSION

Horace Hills Irvine was never governor, but the swanky mansion he built (for $57,000) in the 1910s along historic Summit Avenue in St. Paul is today the official Minnesota Governor's Residence. Donated in the 1960s, the fenced-off acre that includes an impressive terrace and garden out back is very much the current governor's home.

And just as you don't want anyone walking through your living room anytime they want, the Governor's Residence is open only occasionally for tours. Keep an eye on the website for dates; the holiday tours are especially popular. That's when the house's seven bedrooms, ten bathrooms, and nine fireplaces are decorated by various designers from across Minnesota.

Minnesota Governor's Residence, 1006 Summit Ave., St. Paul
www.mn.gov/admin/governors-residence/

VISIT THE
MODEL RAILROAD MUSEUM

Why are model railroads so mesmerizing? The cars go by, the miniature gates go up and down, the signals turn on and off, and then it's an hour later. Thus sums up your next trip to the Twin City Model Railroad Museum, which has been transfixing St. Paulites since 1934.

Formerly housed inside Bandana Square, the museum in 2016 moved to a new site on Transfer Road, near a former Amtrak depot. The main attraction is a large and amazingly detailed O-scale model of the Twin Cities, featuring the mills, depots, and rail yards of yore (the Stone Arch Bridge is depicted when it was a train crossing!).

Staffed by a volunteer cadre of train buffs, it's hard to distinguish the bigger kids in this hobby wonderland.

Twin City Model Railroad Museum
668 Transfer Rd., St. Paul
651-647-9628, www.tcmrm.org

NOTE
To see full-size trains on display, head to the Minnesota Transportation Museum and Jackson Street Roundhouse in St. Paul, or take a road trip to the Lake Superior Railroad Museum in Duluth.

THEY ALL DANCE
AT SHAKOPEE WACIPI

For a celebration of Native American culture, be sure to head to the annual Shakopee Wacipi, or powwow.

Wacipi—the Dakota language word for "they all dance" — is very much a social gathering. You can see people from across Indian Country participating in drum circles and dances in full regalia (don't call them costumes, please).

This particular event, which takes place on the Wacipi grounds near the Mystic Lake Casino Hotel in Shakopee, is also a contest powwow, meaning dancers compete in several categories. It's a beautiful day of song, dance, and ceremony.

The Wacipi Grounds are on tribal lands of the Shakopee Mdewakanton Sioux Community, one of eleven such Native American reservations in Minnesota. Some elements of a wacipi are spiritual for the Dakota people, so be respectful. But most of all, enjoy the community!

Shaokpee Wacipi, 3212 Dakotah Pkwy., Shakopee
www.shakopeedakota.org/culture/wacipi-pow-wow

BEHOLD, THE DIORAMA!
AT THE BELL MUSEUM OF NATURAL HISTORY

Dioramas might have been a more popular art form in the early 1900s, but a visit to the Bell Museum of Natural History reveals a stark truth: when done well, they are meticulous marvels of craftsmanship.

The Bell dates back more than one hundred forty years, and behind the scenes its collection of millions of plant and animal specimens are crucial for research. But the museum's public face is the incredible dioramas from the '40s and '50s that showcase Minnesota's rich and diverse wildlife habitat. From the extinct (passenger pigeon) to the thriving (black bears, squirrels, heron, and deer) and the mysteriously disappearing (moose), visitors come face to face with Minnesota's menagerie in displays that blend painted backgrounds with taxidermy and other elements to complete the foreground.

Then head to the "Touch and See" lab and do just that . . . feel animal hides, antlers, and bones, and see a few live animals also on display, including turtles, tarantulas, and frogs. There's also a planetarium in the building!

Bell has moved to the U's St. Paul campus and features new exhibits (including a wooly mammoth).

The Bell Museum of Natural History, 2088 Larpenteur Ave. W., St. Paul
(on the University of Minnesota St. Paul campus)
612-626-9660, www.bellmuseum.umn.edu

EXPLORE RUSSIAN ART
IN SOUTH MINNEAPOLIS

At first glance, the Museum of Russian Art seems out of place. It's the only museum in North America dedicated to all forms of Russian art, and it's located in the former Mayflower Congregational Church in south Minneapolis, built in the Spanish Colonial Revival style.

So it's a testament to the designers who transformed this building from church to art gallery. The key appears to be a glass-lined mezzanine that allows a second floor of art inside the former main sanctuary space. Here, the ever-changing exhibits will wow you with glances inside Russia during the time of Peter the Great or the czars or the Soviet era or Putin. It's a good place to put away stereotypes you have of the country and its long history and gain a new perspective.

You can also visit the basement gallery and second-floor gift shop, where you can stock up on matryoshka dolls and Russian tea.

The Museum of Russian Art, 5500 Stevens Ave. S., Minneapolis
612-821-9045, www.tmora.org

AMERICAN SWEDISH
INSTITUTE

If lutefisk (item #72) doesn't make you Scandinavian enough, head to the American Swedish Institute in Minneapolis. There's old and new there, and you don't have to be Swedish to appreciate it.

The old is the 1908 Turnblad Mansion, an impressively ornate home along a stretch of Park Avenue once known as the city's "Golden Mile" for its abundance of mansions. The Turnblads lived there briefly before the house became the American Swedish Institute in 1929. The rooms showcase ever-changing exhibits on the culture and traditions of all things Sweden, but the house is its own attraction. Find all eleven porcelain tile stoves (a.k.a. fireplaces), and don't miss the Visby window, an impressive stained glass image that highlights your trip up the grand staircase. And imagine hosting your own party in the second floor ballroom, complete with a stage and skylight.

As for the new, the swanky Nelson Cultural Center houses Fika, a highly regarded restaurant that serves all your favorite Swedish fare. No, the Swedish chef doesn't work there, but the ASI is fit for a king. Sweden's King Carl Gustav visited in 2012.

American Swedish Institute, 2600 Park Ave. S., Minneapolis
612-871-4907, www.asimn.org

SEE THE DRAGON BOAT RACES
ON LAKE PHALEN

A hallmark of the two-day Dragon Festival in St. Paul each summer is the dragon boat races on Lake Phalen. An homage to an ancient Chinese tradition, the impressive forty-foot boats have exquisitely carved and colorful dragon heads and tails at each end. Each boat seats twenty—eighteen paddlers, a drummer, and a flag catcher. The drummer sets a rhythm for the paddlers.

The flag catcher lies belly down on top of the dragon head at the front of the boat and eternally reaches for the flag at the end of the sprint. The first team to catch the flag wins that heat, and several rounds of elimination ensue over the two-day regatta.

Once you've seen the races in person, consider joining a team next year! And don't just come for the races. The entire festival is a showcase of traditional dance and music that will brighten your summer.

Dragon Boat Races, Dragon Festival, Lake Phalen, St. Paul
www.dragonfestival.org

TOUR ST. PAUL'S CAVES
AT WABASH STREET CAVES

St. Paul's riverfront is lined with towering bluffs that offer great views of downtown when you stand on top of them. But what if you stood *inside* the bluffs? There's a network of caves in St. Paul from the days when the bluffs' limestone was mined. Most caves are off-limits for safety reasons, but there's at least one place where you can take a safe tour to get a taste of cave life in St. Paul.

Head over to Wabasha Street Caves on St. Paul's West Side. The building there is built into the bluff and has weekend tours. That's where you'll learn that in addition to mining, these caves were once used to grow mushrooms, store cheese, and help brewers. And St. Paul also has a notorious gangster history; some of these caves doubled as speakeasies.

Wabash Street Caves, 215 Wabasha St. S., St. Paul
651-224-1191, www.wabashastreetcaves.com

GET LOST
IN THE MINNEAPOLIS
INSTITUTE OF ART

There's no good way to describe the enormity of the Minneapolis Institute of Art (now referred to as "Mia," pronounced "MEE-ah"). With its long, sweeping galleries and hallways, it sometimes feels downright Louvre-like. The building itself is also an impressive landmark.

Find artifacts, paintings, photographs, and sculptures spanning six thousand years of cultural history. If you don't like the art in this room, just walk to the next one. There's something for everyone here, from ancient Chinese Buddhist art, a world-renowned Japanese art collection, and an exhibit of Prairie School-style architecture, to the latest work from Minnesota artists, to the annual Art in Bloom show. It's okay to get lost; wear walking shoes. Admission is free (suggested donations accepted at the door), and while most art is hands-off, it's a family-friendly outing.

Minneapolis Institute of Art, 2400 3rd Ave. S., Minneapolis
612-870-3000, www.artsmia.org

PRO TIP

Several points along the north side of the building have floor-to-ceiling windows that offer perfect views of the downtown Minneapolis skyline. There's also an old Otis elevator installed in 1930 that still functions today. Use it! After being inside, consider a walk outside on the MIA grounds along with MCAD (Minneapolis College of Art and Design) and Washburn Fair Oaks Park next door.

CAPONI ART PARK

It's a special treat to find diamonds among the strip malls and copy-and-paste subdivisions of the suburbs. One such gem is a sixty-acre park in Eagan called Caponi Art Park.

Named for its founder, the late artist Anthony Caponi, the park is an eclectic mix of being the Caponis' actual backyard (his wife, Cheryl, still lives on the property); a hidden woods with hiking trails to get away from it all; a series of Caponi-made outdoor sculptures to add to the art of nature; an amphitheater in the woods to enjoy performances; and a scenic overlook with views of both Twin Cities' downtowns.

Open seasonally from May through October, the art park is a free getaway (donations encouraged) from the hustle of the cities and burbs. It's also one of those rare occasions when one man turned over his land to the masses in a space both artists and naturalists will treasure.

Caponi Art Park, 1220 Diffley Rd., Eagan
651-454-9412, www.caponiartpark.org

NOTE

Unlike the ever-changing Franconia Scuplture Park (item #23) or the compact, urban Minneapolis Scuplture Garden (#77), the art pieces at Caponi are more subtle and weaved into a landscape of a heavily wooded terrain. It's almost like nature made the sculptures, too, and placed them right next to that tree. Also, the entrance on Diffley Road sneaks up on you.
Slow down!

JAMES J. HILL HOUSE

When it was completed in 1891, the James J. Hill House was the largest home in Minnesota. It had thirteen bathrooms, twenty-two fireplaces, sixteen chandeliers, and a two-story art gallery—but who's counting? This was a man who could afford to live in luxury. James J. Hill was a railroad baron forever tied to the Great Northern Railway and known in his day as "the Empire Builder" (and a mansion builder, apparently).

This monument to the Gilded Age passed from the Hill family to the Catholic Church for fifty years before the Minnesota Historical Society bought it. Keep in mind that it's a 36,000-square-foot house. The guided tours last seventy-five minutes. So much to see! You can also visit the art gallery without being on the tour.

James J. Hill House, 240 Summit Ave., St. Paul
651-297-2555, www.mnhs.org/hillhouse

PRO TIP

After your tour, take a leisurely walk along historic Summit Avenue to admire St. Paul's mansion row.

TAKE MOVIE-WATCHING TO NEW HEIGHTS
AT HEIGHTS THEATER

You get a sense of what a big deal going to the movies used to be when you head to Heights Theater in suburban Columbia Heights. Built in 1926, the theater was restored in the late 1990s after falling into disrepair. It now screens both first-run and classic films.

It's hard to concentrate on the movies, what with those gorgeous chandeliers to look at—or perhaps the Wurlitzer pipe organ that is played before screenings. Another piano is in the lobby for good measure. Step back into another age, and appreciate the glory of a great historic theater.

Heights Theater, 3951 Central Ave. NE, Columbia Heights
763-789-4992, www.heightstheater.com

CRAWL AND WHIRL
AT ST. PAUL CRAWL AND ART-A-WHIRL

Two more musts in your art endeavoring in the Twin Cities are the St. Paul Art Crawl in Lowertown and Art-A-Whirl in northeast Minneapolis. Both aim to showcase a lot of art in a concentrated area.

In St. Paul, the Lowertown area has been an artist's haven even when the neighborhood was in the dumps. The Art Crawl dates back to the '70s and now features hundreds of artists showcasing their work to tens of thousands of visitors over a weekend. Take the Green Line LRT there, and spend the day walking amidst the art.

Organizers of Art-A-Whirl proclaim their event the largest open studio tour in the country. With the abundance of old factory space that's been made into art studios, northeast Minneapolis is another artists' haven. And this weekend event, usually in May, invites thousands of people to studios, galleries, and storefronts.

There's a lot of art to be seen at both of these events; you'll appreciate the Twin Cities art scene so much more after attending both.

St. Paul Art Crawl, Lowertown, St. Paul
www.saintpaulartcrawl.org

Art-A-Whirl
www.nemaa.org/art-a-whirll
651-297-2555, www.mnhs.org/hillhouse

SHOPPING AND FASHION

VISIT A FARMERS MARKET

Minnesota's shorter growing season is not a barrier to a robust number of farmers markets that have exploded in number in recent years. So grab your canvas bag and plan a weekend morning at a farmers market to fully stock your pantry and meet the farmers who grew your grub. The Minneapolis Farmers Market is a large gathering of vendors wedged in next to a highway and a Catholic Basilica. You'll find produce, flowers, crafts, and baked goods. Even live music! The St. Paul Farmers market next to the new St. Paul Saints ballpark in Lowertown is another must, as are several Twin Cities neighborhoods that have their own smaller markets. And there are several winter markets too.

Minneapolis Farmers Market, 312 E. Lyndale Ave. N., Minneapolis
612-333-1718, www.mplsfarmersmarket.com

St. Paul Farmers Market, 290 5th St. E., St. Paul
651-227-8101, www.stpaulfarmersmarket.com

A grassroots effort to track all the farmers markets around
www.twincitiesfarmersmarkets.com/the-markets/

PICK AND EAT
THE BEST-TASTING APPLES
IN THE WORLD

What a wholesome idea: put your family in the minivan and spend an afternoon picking apples that you spend the next month concocting into all assortments of apple-themed entrees, pies, and fritters. But this isn't just a piece of Americana—this is a hearty hat tip to Minnesota, a state rich in apple tradition.

Not only do the state's apple farmers produce millions of apples a year, some of the most beloved apple varieties were developed in the labs of the University of Minnesota, including Honeycrisp and SweeTango. Apples grow really well in Minnesota, so embrace that, gather the kids, and spend a late summer or fall weekend in an orchard, picking your apple bounty.

Directory of Apple Orchards
www.minnesotagrown.com/member-directory/

GO GLOBAL
AT MIDTOWN GLOBAL MARKET

Visit Mexico, East Africa, Vietnam, and the Middle East at once at the Midtown Global Market at Lake St. and Chicago Ave. in Minneapolis. Housed on the first floor of a repurposed former Sears office building, the market draws shoppers aplenty seeking to catch a meal or stock up for their own pantries.

The Twin Cities has a great assortment of foods from all corners of the earth, but few places feature so many corners in one place. Just strolling through the market is worth it for the pleasant smells.

Both markets and counter-service stores are assembled in one area. Falafel, pasta, and bubble tea for lunch with a locally made draft beer to chase? Sure! Why not? Then stop by the non-food stores to see clothing, crafts, and jewelry from across the globe.

Midtown Global Market, 920 E. Lake St., Minneapolis
612-872-4040, www.midtownglobalmarket.org

FIND STUFF YOU NEVER KNEW YOU NEEDED
AT AX-MAN

For more than fifty years, Ax-Man Surplus has been a must to explore the limits of what can be bought and sold in the commercial market. Need a four-foot red rubber band? Or a beer visor? Or just a huge bag of beads or an inflatable pencil? Ax-Man might have it today, though not necessarily tomorrow.

As they note on their website, Ax-Man "might not have what you need, but we have what you want." Any amount of industrial or electronic surplus or just the stuff in your grandfather's basement is all fair game to be bought and sold. Ax-Man has four locations: St. Paul, St. Louis Park, Fridley, and Crystal.

Ax-Man Surplus
651-646-8653, www.ax-man.com

(ROLLER) COAST
AT THE MALL OF AMERICA

The gargantuan Mall of America is a collection of shopping and superlatives. One of the largest tourist attractions in the world with forty million annual visitors, just to start. But as plentiful as the more than five hundred twenty stores (with no sales tax on clothes in Minnesota) and fifty restaurants are, don't let those be the only reasons you go to MOA. On seven acres of floor space in the middle of the mall is the Nickelodeon Universe amusement park. Parents, you'll love having an indoor place to take your kids in the winter. Ride the Log Chute and then giggle afterward at the photos taken of you just before the start of the final drop.

Mall of America, 60 E. Broadway, Bloomington
952-883-8800, www.mallofamerica.com

PRO TIP

The mall is built on the former Metropolitan Stadium, the Minnesota Twins' first home. Look for home plate, then look along the walls for the one remaining stadium seat that marks where slugger Harmon Killebrew once parked a 522-foot home run in 1967.

TAKE
TO THE OPEN STREETS!

Both Minneapolis and St. Paul have experimented with making streets just a little less about cars, which has included changes like bike lanes but also wholesale, daylong closures of long stretches of busy streets to all vehicles.

The series is called Open Streets; each city has its own take. They're different from festivals and other concert-like events that *happen to require* street closures because, with Open Streets, the act of closing the street *is* the focus. Bike, skate, or just walk about to be more in touch with your neighborhood. It's really about mingling as much as anything.

Major thoroughfares, such as Lyndale, Franklin, Lowry in Minneapolis, and University in St. Paul, have come in for closure during these events. Grab your bike helmet or walking shoes and close the street! Or rather, open it . . . to you!

Open Streets Mpls
www.openstreetsmpls.com

GET A SHAVE, A SHINE,
AND A SHIRT AT HEIMIE'S

You can't help but feel treated like royalty when you step into Heimie's Haberdashery in downtown St. Paul. Descendants of the original Heimie's Menswear that opened in the 1910s operate this updated version of full-service store with an old-school feel. Suits, shirts, and trousers are made to order, but stop by for a shoeshine and a trim at the barbershop. Let the haberdashers at Heimie's walk you through the process of learning what it takes to know your shirts. There's pretty much a 100% guarantee you'll look even better when you leave.

Heimie's Haberdashery, 400 St. Peter St., St. Paul
651-224-2354, www.heimies.com

SUGGESTED
ITINERARIES

DOWNTOWN MINNEAPOLIS RIVERFRONT

Ditch the Car for Nice Ride MN, 51

Find the End of the Endless Bridge, 95

Appreciate the River at the Mississippi National River
    and Recreation Area, 54

Get Your Movie Fix at an Actual Movie Theater, 18

Ruin a Day at Mill City Museum, 90

Span the Stone Arch Bridge, 89

Cheer on the Runners at the Twin Cities Marathon, 64

DOWNTOWN ST. PAUL

Ditch the Car for Nice Ride MN, 51

Bruce Vento Nature Sanctuary, 71

Visit a Farmers Market, 128

Minnesota Children's Museum, 103

Minnesota History Center, 101

Science Museum of Minnesota, 104

Tour the State Capitol, 96

Ride the Rails for a Twin (and Saint) Bill, 22

A COZY SUMMER EVENING OUTDOORS

STATE FAIR

FESTIVALS
BY SEASON

SPRING

Crawl and Whirl at St. Paul Crawl and Art-A-Whirl, 125

Celebrate Cinco de Mayo in the West Side, 43

Get Your Movie Fix at an Actual Movie Theater, 18

SUMMER

Tour Both Cities by Bike on Consecutive Weekends, 55

See the Dragon Boat Races on Lake Phalen, 116

Have a Grand Old Day, 25

Hmong Freedom Celebration, 26

See How Many Fringe Shows You Can Pack In at the
   Minnesota Fringe Festival, 24

Feel the Northern Spark at Northern Spark, 40

AUTUMN

Spend Halloween in the Woods, 30

Go Medieval at the Renaissance Festival, 34

WINTER

Get into the Christmas Spirit at St. Olaf, 41

Play Some Old-Fashioned Hockey at the
   U.S. Pond Hockey Championships, 17

ACTIVITIES
BY SEASON

SPRING

SUMMER

AUTUMN

WINTER

• •

INDEX